Being a Catholic

# MOTHER

redemptorist
publications

# Contents

"There are two lasting bequests
we give our children. The first is roots
and the second is wings."

W. Hodding Carter, author

# Foreword

My seven-year-old son started at his new Catholic school recently. He ran out at the end of his first day, eagerly clutching his new timetable, and waved it in my face.

> *"Mummy, Mummy – guess what – I don't have to go to Mass on Sundays anymore!"*

Great, I thought. He has only been in there five minutes and he is already thinking of lapsing.

> *"And why is that, darling?" I inquired, gently.*

> *"Because we have to go to school Mass on Thursdays!"*

So I took a deep breath and pointed out that in fact he still needed to go at the weekends and that it was a big blessing to be able to go during the week as well. His shoulders drooped a little. He was not convinced.

A classic "Catholic mother" moment. Having been given the lovely task of writing an introduction to *Redemptorist Publications'* lovely manual for Catholic mums, I have had reason to reflect on many other moments, and to consider the challenges that face all of us as we struggle to do the right thing by our children in a fast-changing world which our Catholic grandmothers would barely recognise.

I married, very happily, seventeen years ago – but, like many, to a non-Catholic husband.

Even before our children were a twinkle in our eyes, it meant some pretty frank conversations about how we would be raising a family. To be a Catholic mother would only work with my husband's support: the baptisms, confessions, first holy communions – not to mention weekly Mass. For an outsider, it is a formidable prospect. Thankfully, he accepted it and still does. And although not a regular Mass-goer, he has got involved in parish life – appreciating the sense of community it builds around our children and family life. It is in the midst of that parish life, I think, that many of us find our feet as Catholic mums, whether or not we are married to Catholics, or are, perhaps, single mothers. I made one of my best friends while standing at the back of church during Mass, as our toddler boys rolled about on the floor and ran around outside in the car park when they were making too much noise. You quickly develop a bit of an in-church support network, where the lines between families are blurred. As our children grew, so did we, as mothers. Only another mother gets it, when you roll your hollowed eyes at the family Mass on a Sunday morning after another night of broken sleep. We have supported one another and exchanged glances of anxiety as the children went into school for the first time. But we have also shared many moments of pride – silently cheering on one another's children on their first day as altar servers, or when they have climbed the sanctuary steps to read at the school Mass.

But what I never quite reckoned with is how much your children teach you. I have discovered previously untapped and unknown reserves of patience and stamina. When it comes to talking to your children about your faith, it makes you examine very carefully what it is you actually believe. Explaining the basics to a child forces you to go back to the very roots of your own faith. This is sometimes a tough process, but it can nurture you as well as your child: the joy of Christmas, Easter, first holy communion – all seen through fresh eyes – is truly invigorating. There will, no doubt, be many of you who will be saying at this point, "Ha! Just you wait until they are teenagers." I am aware that the most challenging years of motherhood for me lie just around the corner. But if we mothers keep talking, sharing and supporting one another – and, crucially, do not lose our sense of humour – with the grace of God, there is little that we cannot tackle.

**Julie Etchingham**
*is a TV news reader and journalist.*

# *Introduction –* Welcome, whoever you are

"Being a **mother** is a huge part of my identity. Because I am **Catholic** all through – like a stick of rock – it is difficult to separate the two."

Morag, mother of five

6

The first thing to say to you is that you and your story belong in the pages of this book.

You may be a mother-to-be, or just embarking on the adventure of motherhood with a newborn. You may have toddlers, young children, teens, twenty-somethings or older, or any combination of the above. Your ties with your child or children might be biological, or you might be a foster or stepmother. You might live in a family situation or be a single parent for one of a number of reasons – you might be divorced, separated, widowed or unmarried. You may, very sadly, have lost a child through bereavement or estrangement – none of that makes you any less a mother.

Just as your personal circumstances are unique, so is your faith. Whether you are a "cradle" Catholic, a "lapsed" Catholic, a regular churchgoer, or simply curious about the Catholic faith, please know that this book is for you. The point is that, if any part of this book does not resonate with you, or even leaves you with a pang of envy, anger, regret or sadness, please forgive it any insensitivity and refuse to feel discouraged. Be assured that you are included and welcome, and that this reassuring message is echoed by the worldwide Catholic Church!

Whatever your circumstances, you are very likely holding this book now because you are a Catholic who is also a mother – although perhaps you see yourself more as a mother who happens to be Catholic.

As Catholics we often hear more about fathers than mothers. We have a Father God and we call our priests "Father". Few would deny, however, the powerful and abiding influence of mothers – as demonstrated by the Blessed Virgin Mary – or that a mother's love endures far beyond the cradle, childhood, adolescence and teenage years. Its critical importance is evidenced over and over again in research, as well as our lived experience.

So what does it mean to you, to be a Catholic mother? Does it mean welcoming a limitless number of children into your family? Does it mean bringing up your children to consider a future as a priest or a nun? Does it mean referring all the decisions in your home life to Church teaching and practice? Does it mean, as it does for Morag (see quote opposite), that your Catholic faith and the rest of your life are so close-knit that they cannot be distinguished?

How does being a Catholic mother fit in a society which seems to have largely turned its back on religion and faith? What can we do to mother our children in the Catholic tradition when there are just so many other demands on our time and energy? And what does it mean anyway to mother "in the Catholic tradition"?

In this book Catholic mothers share their thoughts on juggling motherhood, faith, God, home, church and that perennial guilt that comes with it all. Their varied responses colour the following pages.

"The other mothers make me feel **less alone.** The praying reminds me that **God is in charge** and can sort everything out. **Thankfully.**"

Karen, mother of two

## Meditations and reflections – touching base with ourselves

As a mother, by definition you have a busy life. At various points in this book you will find sections entitled "Meditation", "Reflection" or "Heartbeat meditation". These are designed to help you, amid the noise and busyness, to quickly touch base with God, yourself, and your priorities. While they are quick and easy, they still take discipline and practice. So get into the habit, when you feel stressed, fatigued or negative in any way, of recognising how you feel and allowing yourself a moment of meditation. Over time you will find it makes a world of difference!

## Talking it through – touching base with other people

As we get into the rhythm of motherhood we are often so busy and distracted that we lose sight of real, meaningful connections with other people. We might get to know plenty of other mothers socially, but if we are not attentive to them they never deepen as friendships. The "Talking it through" sections are suggested conversation starters to get you talking, particularly with mothers, on matters of faith.

You might read them and think, "That's all very well, but I would never dream of starting a conversation about God with another mother – not even one I know from church." Sure, initiating a conversation might involve a bit of social awkwardness or embarrassment, but motherhood brings us closer to God in a very elemental, raw way – you might be surprised who might be glad of an opportunity to open up and talk. We all yearn so deeply to express our spiritual side. This is not about evangelisation, or getting on a soap box, but about reaching out to seek and offer spiritual support.

These conversations are not about finding answers – only we can work out what is best in our own situation. Making deeper connections is what really matters, because being curious about God and one another keeps us alive to our faith and ourselves.

## Prayers –
## touching base with God

You will also find prayers throughout the book. Short and to the point, they suggest ways of giving thanks, expressing joy, doubt or fear – whatever you are feeling in the moment. Feel free to adapt them to your circumstances. They are there to help you open the channels of communication with God. Again, this is all about getting into habits. Over time you will find that a few snatched moments of prayer in a day add up to far more than the sum of their parts, leaving you with a greater sense of peace.

## Prayer, reflection and discussion

These practical responses – prayer, reflection and discussion – are at the core of this book. Whatever challenges God sends our way, if we get into the habit of responding with prayer, reflection and discussion, we are allowing ourselves to learn from and engage with God, ourselves and the world. With practice, we will become calmer and better able to cope with the everyday stresses and strains of motherhood. We may also find that our choices are wiser and better informed.

The exercises in the book are designed to be easy and to fit into a mother's busy day – but, even so, they take discipline, and that should not be underestimated. When we are on the "hamster wheel" of our daily routines, our instinct is simply to keep going. So start by noticing those times when you do have a minute in which you could pause for reflection, yet choose not to. You might find that you have more time than you thought!

As we enable our children to grow and develop and teach them about faith, it is every bit as important that we grow and develop ourselves – as mothers and women – and in our faith. It matters, not just for practical purposes, but because God longs for us to know God better.

"The availability of a father or mother to their children is so important: 'waste time' with your children, play with your children."

Pope Francis

### A prayer
### of thanksgiving

Dear Lord, this is fantastic –
you really know what is best for
us. Thank you from the bottom of
my heart. I am sorry for the times
I did not trust you. Help me
to remember this moment
next time I doubt your
providence. Amen.

## Before you begin

Look at these comments from Catholic mothers. They point to the ups and downs, the efforts and joys of living a faithful life, and a sense that mothering children of whatever age is closely intertwined with God's own creative life. Notice especially the depth of feeling in their words. What does that say to you about motherhood, particularly from a spiritual perspective?

### Being a mother...

"… has been one of the greatest but, at times, also the most painful experience of my life."

"There have been many times when I felt that I had not been prepared to be a mother. It sometimes feels as though it is a life of drudgery with no breaks or treats."

"… is the most challenging, rewarding, frustrating, important, exhausting and emotionally satisfying role I have ever undertaken."

"… is wonderful, challenging, exhausting, uplifting."

### Being a Catholic mother...

"… means I can get the help and strength to come through the most painful and distressing situations."

"… means that I have taken very seriously my promises to raise my children in the faith and to send them to Catholic schools."

"… has meant that I should be willing to make sacrifices and provide my child with a moral grounding."

"… helps me to know that God plays a very big part in the upbringing of the children and that I have been given the auspicious task of bringing up three of God's children."

"God is a Father, but even more, a Mother."

Pope John Paul I

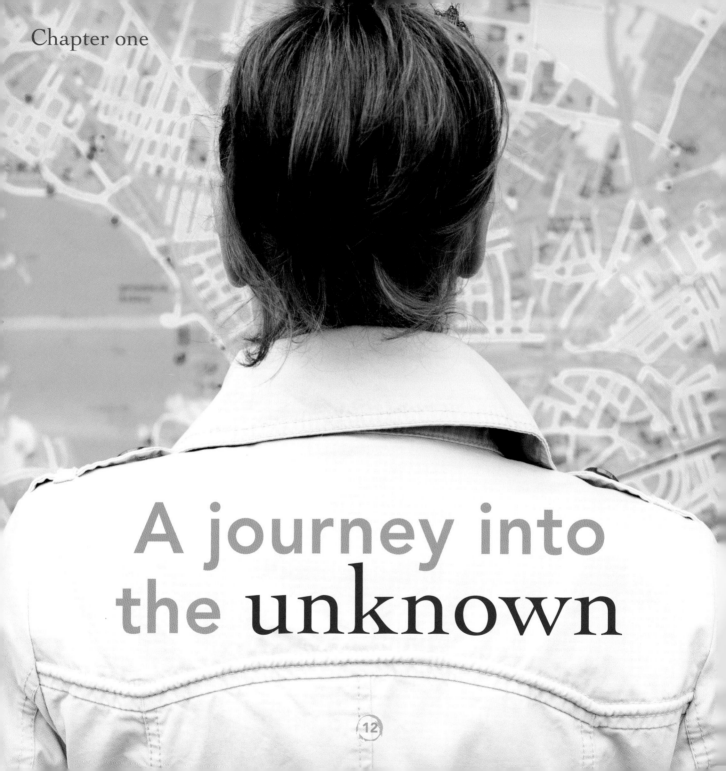

# Chapter one

# A journey into the unknown

> "Before I formed you in the
> womb I knew you."
>
> Jeremiah 1:5

Just for now let us assume that you are a first-time mother with a newborn baby. If not, just backtrack to the birth of your first child and remember how you felt at the time. For many mothers it is a combination of physical exhaustion and a rush of joy, peace and the most overpowering love.

Along with a new person in your life, and your new identity as a mother, you have a whole new set of challenges to face – challenges that will last a lifetime and need time to settle into your heart, your daily life and your faith. So go easy on yourself, recognise the enormous scale of what has happened, and, above all, pray – and keep praying – for God's guidance over the coming days, weeks, months, years and decades.

Motherhood is a journey into the unknown. Once conception has taken place there is no knowing what will happen. Will my baby be healthy? Will I cope once he or she arrives? There is really no getting away from just how awesome a responsibility motherhood is – which is what makes it one of life's great faith adventures.

Yet for all the uncertainties, motherhood also brings unparalleled joy, delight and awe. After the sight and smell of a newborn, come the sticky wet toddler kisses and the heavy sweetness of sleepy children, the exhilaration of birthdays and Christmas (once the work is done!), and the journey through many firsts – friendships, boyfriends, girlfriends, jobs and homes – until suddenly the day dawns when we realise our children are independent adults.

Motherhood is a spiritual journey which, if we embrace it as such, leads us to a deeper appreciation of the heart of God, who is both mother and father to us all. For the heart of God is love. And in all the ups and downs of motherhood, we come to understand better the demands of loving others. We also discover the extent to which God truly loves us.

### A prayer during pregnancy:

Creator God, your new life is growing inside me. Help my baby to grow healthy and well. Help me to adjust and learn how to protect and nurture (him/her). Hold me close when my labour starts, and give me strength to endure its demands. Help me to welcome my child just as (he/she) is, and as (he/she) will become all the days of (his/her) life. I place my trust and hope in you.
Amen.

### Heartbeat meditation

Simply close your eyes and become aware of the next two breaths you take. Understand that the Holy Spirit is present in those breaths, and thank God for the gift of your life and for the life you have co-created.

# " TALKING IT THROUGH

- What were your hopes and fears during pregnancy?

- How did things turn out?

- What, for you, was the biggest surprise? Or joy? Or relief?

- What did you learn from your experience? "

**A prayer for birth:**

Loving God, thank you for this baby, so fresh and so familiar. Thank you for the wonder that (he/she) is and for entrusting (him/her) to my care. Thank you for the happiness I see in those around my child. Thank you for everyone who has helped us to get this far.
Amen.

# Chapter two

# Staging posts

"Joys – their health and development. Their striving for ambitions in sport, education and professional life. Their decency and strong sense of morality and social justice. Has my faith made a difference? – Yes, prayer is a huge comfort and source of inspiration – so is the knowledge of a God who is interested in our affairs and loves each one of us just as we are."

Sophie, mother of two

Motherhood is like a game of snakes and ladders. Just when you think you have reached the top of a ladder – your children are flourishing and their lives are going smoothly – suddenly something unexpected happens, everything unravels and you land with a bump at the bottom of a snake. It is even more demanding with children at different stages – some of us negotiate the "terrible twos" and the teenage years simultaneously!

As you duck and dive your way through your particular experience of motherhood, you might find that the following "staging posts" help you to stop and reflect, and to see how many opportunities there are for you to grow spiritually amid all the chaos.

## Welcoming

"Whoever welcomes this child in my name welcomes me,
and whoever welcomes me welcomes the one who sent me."

Luke 9:48

Babies come with baggage – mountains of the stuff: nappies, bottles, buggies, cots and car seats, to name just a few of the things you find yourself weighed down with. Often making room for a new life means having a good clear out, which is just the beginning of a lifetime of adjustments that a mother makes. But a baby's smile can cut through all the clutter, and in those precious moments a mother does not find welcoming a new life any hardship at all.*

This is not only about welcoming and accommodating a child in the world, but also about embracing the new experiences that come with parenthood – both the easy ones and those we find challenging. It is also about keeping that welcome alive for a lifetime – even when it is not always reciprocated. It can be a real challenge, for example, to keep welcoming your sullen teenager when he shuts you out of his life and slams the door of his room, making you feel like an intruder in his life.

**A prayer for
a mother who feels
shut out of her child's life**

Jesus, who made room for everyone around your table, teach me to welcome and keep an unconditional welcome alive. At the same time, Lord, teach me not to shut others out. Amen.

*It must be acknowledged that some mothers, for whatever reason, do struggle with bonding with their baby. If you identify with that you are not alone. There are plenty of professionals, including your GP, who can help – please seek their support as soon as possible.

## Nurturing

> "Is there anyone among you who, if your child asks for bread, will give a stone? Or if the child asks for a fish, will give a snake?"
>
> Matthew 7:9-10

A baby has very basic needs – milk, warmth, shelter and love. As a baby grows, his or her needs become more complex. Just as he or she needs nutrition for physical growth, babies also need sustenance for emotional and spiritual growth, and a healthy immune system to help cope with the trials of life.

We could no more control our child's emotional and spiritual development than we could force him or her to grow taller. (Yet it is astonishing how many of us, when we are faced with a real and alarming situation, resort to the equivalent of doing just that!) God the creator is at work in our children's bodies and also in their spirits. Our responsibility as parents is to ensure that their body, mind and soul are well nourished to allow for healthy growth.

## Binding

In the same way that a binding holds the pages of this book together and in the right order, mothers attend to the binding within a family: bringing together squabbling children, facilitating a truce, helping to see that no relationship goes irreversibly wrong. The quality of the binding is important: it should keep everything together, but not be restrictive. This is a hugely important role, and one that a mother spends her entire life perfecting.

We are called to be brothers and sisters in Christ, and this is something we start to learn through family life. Whenever we say the Creed we affirm our faith in the three persons of the Trinity. The relationship between God the Father, God the Son and God the Holy Spirit is the model for the binding of our own family relationships – absolutely united yet distinct.

As our children go to school and develop their own friendships, they become part of a wider community. At this point a mother's binding role changes, but the same skills are called for in a different way. As she takes a step back from her child's life, her vision becomes wider and encompasses more. Being a caring presence in the lives of our children's friends as they grow, for example, is an enormously important part of mothering, as is knowing that our child is cared for, loved and held in the world, as he or she is at home.

"Our personality develops in the family, by growing up with our mum and dad, our brothers and sisters, by breathing in the warmth of the home."

Pope Francis

**A prayer for a mother who feels the binding is falling apart**

Lord, keep before me the example of your Holy Trinity – Father, Son and Holy Spirit. Bind my family together in love and guide me in my role as unifier.
Amen.

"As mother, I tune in to each of the individual people in the family, as well as paying attention to the family dynamics. I know myself to be ordinary. When I was young I wanted to be or do something special and I now see that being ordinary is fine. Because of a deep belief and prayer life, I am at my best when at peace and so I can share that with others."

Morag, mother of five

### Surviving

"When I look at my children and take pride in their achievements, I get a small sense of **how God must look at me.**"

Angie, mother of two

For all the advances in medicine and midwifery, during pregnancy and birth we are involved in a very raw and elemental fight for survival – our concern is keeping our baby alive. As our child grows we teach him or her other survival skills: how to cross the road safely, how to use money wisely, whom to speak to or not, how to stay safe online, how to stay healthy and well – the list goes on.

But while we understand that during pregnancy we must take care of our bodies in order that a baby can grow within us, mothers are often less attentive when it comes to their own well-being. It is not unusual for a mother to deplete her own resources as she cares for her children – allowing herself to become frazzled and tired, running on empty, neglecting her own nutritional needs. (How often have you heard a mother say, "I just eat whatever the kids are eating"?)

### Heartbeat meditation

Close your eyes and become aware of your breath. Sense the presence of the Holy Spirit in all the stages of your life, your children's lives, and your family. Take a few breaths as you allow that knowledge to settle deeply into you.

## Watching

"At the Cross her station keeping, stood the mournful mother weeping, close to Jesus to the last."

Part of *Stabat Mater*,
a thirteenth-century Catholic hymn about and to Mary

There are times when all that can be done is to watch and wait. When we have done all we can as mothers to welcome, nurture, bind and save our children, we have to accept our limitations. We watch to see how things will turn out and what more may be asked of us. But watch and wait we must.

These moments are often dark nights of our souls. Perhaps our children have grown up to reject the faith that is important to us. Or perhaps they struggle with depression or have been deeply hurt, or have yet to find a fulfilling vocation.

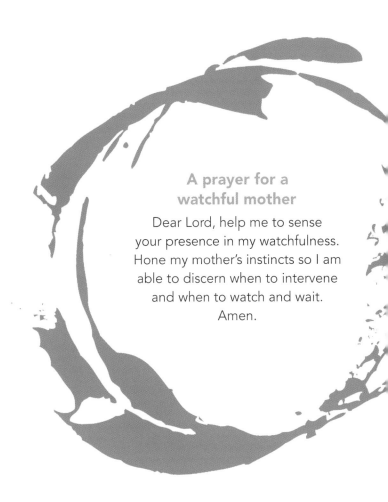

### A prayer for a watchful mother

Dear Lord, help me to sense your presence in my watchfulness. Hone my mother's instincts so I am able to discern when to intervene and when to watch and wait. Amen.

Keeping watch through the night is a long-established Christian practice. We know that Christ himself suffered a similar agony and that his mother Mary kept watch as he was killed. Sometimes the only comfort comes from knowing we do not suffer alone. Even when our watching becomes the pattern of life for years, we are never alone in this. God too, and God's mother, share in our experience.

## 66 TALKING IT THROUGH

- In what way did you have to make room for your child when he or she was born? Did you find it easy or a struggle?

- Describe a time when you felt shut out of your child's life.

- How have you tried to meet your child's spiritual needs?

- What would fulfilling those needs involve?

- What has the Trinity taught you about family relationships?

- Do you sometimes neglect your own needs? If so, what can you do to support your well-being?

- Can you think of a time when you have had no choice but to watch and wait? How did that feel? What helped you then? **99**

"I have also learnt that sometimes we have to relinquish our hold on a child who is determined to go his own way and allow God to take over, even though this may mean a time of hardship and difficulty for the child. This involves a lot of trust that God really does love our child even more than we do and that he wants the best for our child too."

Melanie, mother of four

# Chapter three

# The transforming power
# of motherhood

Motherhood is all about transformation. This is an essential part of spiritual growth. As mothers we find ourselves completely and utterly changed – yet at the same time we remain exactly who we are and always have been. In this way, motherhood is a journey of discovery into our true nature, the core of our being.

## Your relationship with your husband or partner

Along with everything else, motherhood transforms our relationships – with our partner, family, friends and colleagues. A couple's relationship changes fundamentally when they take on the shared responsibility of parenthood. It can bring them much closer together, or it can bring out and highlight differences they may not have known existed. Generally, it does a bit of both.

### Do:

▶ take time to talk.

▶ practise kindness.

▶ try to see each other's point of view. Even if you do not agree, try to understand where your partner is coming from so you can discuss your differences.

### Don't:

▶ underestimate the importance a father has in a child's life.

▶ be tempted to play status games, or "pull rank" as a mother.

## THROUGH THE LENS

Magda and Ben had always agreed about all the big decisions in life, so it came as a shock to realise that they had very different ideas about educating their children. Although Magda only occasionally went to church, she had been raised a Catholic and her childhood grounding in faith was very important to her. Ben on the other hand had no faith background, and felt strongly that the children should not be what he called "indoctrinated" at school, insisting that it would be better if they made up their own minds about religion.

The rows were getting them nowhere, until, in desperation, Magda resorted to prayer – something she had not done since childhood. In those quiet moments, asking for God's guidance, she started to understand that Ben needed his fears allayed and to be shown the real value of faith in a child's life. When she invited him to visit a priest with her to talk it through, she was pleasantly surprised when he agreed. It was the beginning of a new way for them to negotiate as a couple.

## Parents, siblings and in-laws

As Magda and Ben found, the experience of parenthood can highlight differences that we had not been fully aware of. This can also be true of our relationships with our parents, siblings and in-laws. When they shift places in the family tree to become grandparents, uncles and aunts, it invariably opens up a whole new set of challenges for them. Like you, they are embarking on a new journey – unlike you, their role is not clear cut. Working out their new status will inevitably involve some trial and error – and very likely a blunder or two.

So if your mother-in-law is interfering, ask yourself if she is compensating for uncertainty about her role. Or if your father has a know-it-all attitude, could it be his way of dealing with anxiety? Perhaps your indifferent sister is trying to cope with sadness at not having children herself.

Often it can take all your resources of compassion and understanding to handle these relationships with grace, particularly when you are shattered and stressed, or your hormones are in flux. But finding ways of strengthening family ties not only creates lifelong allies for us and our offspring, it is part of building a supportive family network. Rising to these challenges is not only practical mothering, but also a way of actively doing God's will.

### Reflection

Read 1 Corinthians 13, about love. Now close your eyes for five breaths and with the out breath, imagine yourself letting go of any anger or resentment. With the in breath, visualise your heart filling up with love and compassion. Next, think about the important people in your life. As you do so, do you come across any niggles or irritations? Notice what and who they are, and commit to pray about them another time.

### A prayer for compassion

Lord, (he/she) is winding me up again. Yet I know (he/she) means well and loves us all, and I know that you love (him/her) just as (he/she) is. Give me kindness and generosity of spirit, Lord, and thank you for the love that surrounds us.
Amen.

"I am not sure that a 'Catholic mother' is any different from any other mother. My experience of being a mother and observing other mothers is that we want to serve our children, protect and nurture them, however limited we may be. Whatever our shortcomings we do our best."

Bella, mother of five

## New relationships

Time and again, our children drag us out of our comfort zone. For many parents it starts at school age when the bubble of family life is pierced as we start to meet our children's teachers, friends and their friends' parents. Little do our children realise what an impact their social life has on our own.

Do not underestimate how tricky these relationships can be. You might simply not get on with someone. Or you may encounter people whose values and lifestyles may not sit easily with your own. This is a good opportunity to explain your choices and values to your children. How you go about that depends on your circumstances, but here are a few suggestions:

### *Do:*

▶ ask for God's guidance in explaining your values to your children.

▶ be clear about your own values – what is acceptable and what is not.

▶ be clear about the values you share with your husband or partner – take a bit of time to discuss them. Even if you do not agree on something, you do need to adopt a "line" – so negotiate until you find the middle ground.

▶ be prepared to answer unexpected questions – children are good at challenging our assumptions!

### *Don't:*

▶ try to force yourself to like anyone. If you just do not "gel", acknowledge it, pray for wisdom to see them as they really are and know in your heart (if not in your mind) that everyone is a son or daughter of God.

▶ feel you have to accept a behaviour or attitude you do not agree with. Pray for wisdom in deciding whether you should challenge something directly, or indirectly (through your living example), or "live and let live".

## Single motherhood

It goes without saying that being a single mother can be very tough at times. Increasingly, however, the Church acknowledges, supports and celebrates the existence of "patchwork" families, as the story of Anna Romero demonstrates so well (see below).

### THROUGH THE LENS

In 2013, an Italian divorcee, Anna Romero, discovered she was pregnant by a married man. The man tried to persuade her to have an abortion, but Anna made the difficult choice to go it alone and keep her baby. When she was still pregnant, she poured out her heart in a letter to Pope Francis. She addressed the envelope "Pope Francis, the Vatican" and posted it, never for one moment expecting a reply.

Imagine Anna's astonishment, then, when she answered the phone a short while later, and immediately recognised the voice on the other end of the line as that of Pope Francis himself. Talking to her as though she were a dear friend, he reassured Anna that she would never be alone, and reminded her that a child is a gift from God and a sign of divine providence. He commended her for being "brave and strong" for her unborn child.

When Anna shared her fears about baptising her baby because she was divorced and a single mother, the Holy Father assured her that he would be her spiritual father, and even offered to baptise her baby himself.

If you are a single mother, Anna's story should reassure you that you are included, encouraged and supported by the Church. Of course we do not all live out the Gospel as fully as Pope Francis, and you may feel that this encouraging message is not echoed within your parish or church community.

But rather than shrinking into invisibility, could you follow Francis' example? If you can invest the time, think about initiating a scheme yourself. See if you can arrange to meet your priest or someone in your church or parish. If your time is too scarce, you could write down some suggestions as to how things could improve, and start the conversation going. Give some thought as to how you and anyone in a similar position could be helped to become more involved in church life, practically, socially, and spiritually.

"I think there is a huge need for mothers to be affirmed in the work that they are doing. Parenting is a hard slog and I don't think it receives the recognition that it should from the Church. It is a vocation, just as much as the priesthood!"

Melanie, mother of four

## " TALKING IT THROUGH

- In what way has motherhood affected your relationships with others?

- How have your assumptions about other people been challenged by the experience of motherhood?

- Share a story about a time in which you communicated your values to your child. Did it go well? What was his or her reaction?

- What do you know about single motherhood? What practical support does your parish offer? How can you help? "

Perfect
motherhood

"Being a Catholic mother means that I am forced to confront my **failings, weaknesses and imperfections** on a daily basis, and attempt to address them in an **honest and meaningful way** – trying and failing and **trying again.**"

Rebecca, mother of three

Rebecca is absolutely right to realise that motherhood is not about perfection. Thankfully, the 1950s ideal of motherhood has been blown out of the water, and we are given permission to be imperfect, to muddle through motherhood and to make it up as we go along. That is a big relief!

But just pause for a moment to consider – what does "not being perfect" mean to you? For many people perfection is not only an ideal – it is an addiction. Not like drugs or alcohol, but it can be damaging. This might not affect you, but it is worth a mention because it is much more common than you might imagine.

Many of us struggle with letting go of our day-to-day habits, routines and rituals. We might feel relaxed only when the house is thoroughly clean, for example, or when we have balanced the household accounts, or bought the weekly shopping. Everyone has their own idea of "perfection".

Whatever your routines and rituals, your children will challenge them more than anything else you have ever experienced. They will start doing it as, to quote Shakespeare, "mewling and puking" newborns. They will continue as sticky toddlers, attention-seeking ten-year-olds, and as dishevelled and demanding teenagers they will ramp up their efforts, and so on – until, please

God – grandchildren come along to take over disruption duties.

Seriously, if we are perfection addicts in one way or another, having children in our lives can lead to real frustration and set up inner conflict. Something has to give and over time it will. But for many mothers, kicking the habit (in ways we may not even have been aware of) is one of the hardest and most drawn-out sacrifices we will make for our children. We are so attached to our habits – so learning to let them go is a great lesson in faith.

**These are not solutions, but suggestions:**

For the mum who is a household perfectionist and finds it hard to let anyone else do the housework to her high standards:

Write and memorise a quick prayer of acceptance, acknowledging that household chores are – and always will be – ongoing and that family life will only generate more. If it helps, pin it up somewhere visible. Start a family discussion – would a housework rota help you to let go of the feeling that you, and only you, need to do everything?

*Reflection*

Read Luke 10:38-42. Close your eyes and reflect on it. What can you learn from Mary and Martha?

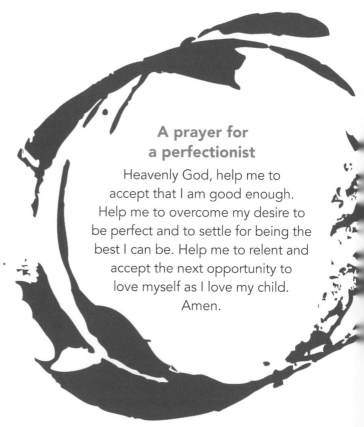

**A prayer for a perfectionist**

Heavenly God, help me to accept that I am good enough. Help me to overcome my desire to be perfect and to settle for being the best I can be. Help me to relent and accept the next opportunity to love myself as I love my child. Amen.

For the mum who is anxious and finds it hard to trust anyone else to look after her children:

Start by talking to God about your anxieties. As you pray, really face them. Chances are you have a fertile imagination and visualise all kinds of disasters befalling your child. You could try running through the scenarios in your head. Give up if you find it too distressing, but you might find that the exercise lays some of them to rest. Lastly, try not to compound your anxiety with a sense of shame. Telling God helps with this; so does discussing it with a sympathetic friend.

For the mum who is a "finisher/completer":

Grazed knees and screeching tantrums are jarring interruptions in anyone's day. You stop and tend to them (you certainly cannot concentrate with that racket going on), while in the background that paperwork is piling up in your in-tray, and the to-do list just seems to be writing itself. Again, it is a matter of learning to accept the imperfect, and again there is no better way to do that than through reflection, discussion and prayer.

### A prayer for a worrier

Gentle Jesus, help me to go easy on myself. Help me to feel your deep and abiding love for me exactly as I am here and now. Help me to find ways to cope with my fears and help me to communicate your reassurance to my child.
Amen.

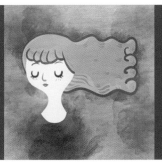

### Heartbeat meditation

Read the story of what happens just after the death of John the Baptist (Mark 6:29-34); see how Jesus reacts on hearing the news (verses 29 to 34). Notice how spiritually supple he is, able to respond to the situation before him and to the needs of the people. When you next get a moment come back to verse 34 and reflect on it. Just by doing that, you will learn from it.

### A prayer for
### a finisher/completer

Lord, these children – grazed
knees and all – are living witnesses
to the perfection of your creation.
I want to learn from the example of
your Son, Lord, and to learn how
to relax and be fully with my
children when they need me.
Amen.

# 66 TALKING IT THROUGH

- What is your idea of perfection? How does motherhood get in the way of that?

- What habits, routines and rituals are you attached to?

- How does it feel not to be able to indulge them?

- Is there any alternative?

- Are there any practical steps you could take that would help you to let go of the feeling that you need to do everything? 99

"I use to run around all the time trying to make everything look perfect: washing all done, ironing all done, house spotless. Now I crochet and knit. It gives me time to relax and think, and to clear my mind. So I am having conversations, simple conversations that I never had time for before. I have made mistakes trying to be everything I thought people wanted me to be and I got it totally wrong."

Louise, mother of two

# Chapter five

# Passing on our *faith*

Of all the responsibilities a Catholic mother has towards her children, passing on the faith is perhaps the most challenging. It is not quite the same as setting boundaries in other aspects of family life, encouraging good manners or making sure your children have nourishing food – or is it?

> "I learned more about Christianity from my mother than from all the theologians in England."
>
> John Wesley, founder of the Methodist Church

> "Without a doubt being a mother has given me more insight into the mystery of God than anything else in my life."
>
> Bella, mother of five

## Your unique "faith print"

How you go about sharing your faith with your children depends on your own starting point. Your "faith print" is as unique as your thumbprint, and this book makes no assumptions about you. The deep mystery of motherhood leads many women to explore the possibilities of faith in new ways – you may be just starting out on a faith journey or rediscovering your long-lost faith, or you may find in motherhood that you are seeing your faith in a new light.

Whatever your story, make it truthful because only then will you be able to pass what is real on to your children. Allow it to be an opportunity to "take stock" of your own faith, your priorities, doubts and niggles. Believe it or not, the Catholic Church really does allow for this and encourages honest enquiry! If, for example, you find you are expected to have your baby baptised simply because it is what you do in your family, remember that baptism is an expression of your faith as a parent (on behalf of your child). Think about it, pray and talk about it. If you have not been to church or confession for a while, it would be a very good idea to go – as long as you do it with an open and enquiring mind. Or if this seems too scary, why not ask to speak to your parish priest "informally". He is there to help.

## Face to faith

We often hear that churchgoing is in decline and congregation numbers are falling. But by God's grace the Church is thriving in many corners of the world. If your family is part of that, enjoy it to the full. Thank God for every time you stand side by side at Mass, or kneel together at the altar rail, for the harmony of your voices singing together, and for every sacrament you share.

But make a clear distinction between feeling proud and being smug – which is a sure sign of dead faith. Jesus frequently spoke about the importance of being vigilant (Matthew 24:42), and your calling as a mother is to ensure that your family's faith life never becomes a dull routine or empty duty. How you go about this depends on your circumstances. Here are some ideas to keep faith alive in your home:

▶ Encourage discussion and debate. It is amazing how often people will talk about anything other than religion – so do not allow it to become a taboo subject. Try to encourage people to share their real feelings – including doubts and concerns. Steer the conversation, but avoid the impulse to censor ideas you do not agree with or find unpalatable. Keep the conversation going until it is an everyday topic of discussion.

▶ Arrange a family visit to a church, cathedral, shrine or religious community. You would be surprised how fascinating children find religious life, and many communities are open to visits, provided you make advance arrangements.

▶ Do you ever do any charitable work as a family, or take part in church activities? If not, give it a go.

▶ What part does prayer play in your life and the lives of your children? If you do not already say grace before meals, or bedtime prayers, consider introducing them.

"Evening prayers often turn into quite a philosophical discussion. We usually start with open prayers, such as 'Who wants to thank God for something?' Quite often this has been the spark of the discussion about, for example, why did Aunty Lorna die when she was such a good person and where has she gone and when will we see her again, and will she remember us? Why did the earthquake have to happen to those people in Haiti? Why was our cousin born needing an operation on his lip? Do Muslims go to heaven too? I find I really have to keep on my toes and read about my faith."

Ruth, mother of four

## Faith no more

If your family is one of the many being challenged by a disruption to the continuity of faith, it can be both upsetting and frightening to see your children rejecting it. Of course it is not a phenomenon limited to your family, but part of a wider, cultural secularisation.

There is an idea that parents whose children turn away from the faith must have done something wrong. But as you will probably have witnessed in other families, attending Mass every Sunday, saying grace before every meal and reading the Bible regularly does not guarantee that children will grow up to be devout Catholics – indeed it seems that piety can have an off-putting effect for some.

The bottom line is that a mother cannot predict the kind of adults her children will become in any respect, let alone in matters of faith. It is part of the marvellous but unnerving mystery of motherhood. Then again, God works in wonderful ways. You may know someone whose child became resolutely anti-Catholic for a while, before turning back to the faith. When someone does embrace faith after a wobble, it is often a deeper, more lasting commitment.

If your children reject your faith, it might help to think of your role as not dissimilar to the Church. Like the Church, you, by being who you are, are able to give your family a sense of connection in terms of place, history and Catholic heritage. Like the Church, sometimes that is all you can do – just be there, be yourself and make it clear that you are ready to talk when the time is right.

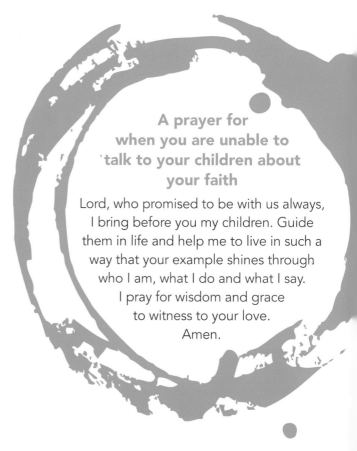

**A prayer for when you are unable to talk to your children about your faith**

Lord, who promised to be with us always, I bring before you my children. Guide them in life and help me to live in such a way that your example shines through who I am, what I do and what I say. I pray for wisdom and grace to witness to your love. Amen.

## The sacraments

"You have asked to have your children (child) baptised. In doing so you are accepting the responsibility of training them (him/her) in the practice of the faith. It will be your duty to bring them (him/her) up to keep God's commandments as Christ taught us, by loving God and our neighbour."

Rite of Baptism of Children

In brief, a sacrament is a sacred rite – although there is far more to it than that. Catholics are unique in celebrating seven sacraments: baptism, Eucharist, reconciliation, confirmation, matrimony, holy orders (when a deacon, priest or bishop is ordained) and anointing of the sick. Sacraments are not only major rituals when God's grace very evidently and powerfully embraces us; they also show us how God continually gives us opportunities for grace in day-to-day life. The sacrament of reconciliation, for example, reminds us of God's love at work in all the forgiving, merciful and reconciling activities of the home.

Baptism is a wonderful way of welcoming someone (who is usually but not always a baby) into the faith community. Like all the sacraments, God works through it in response to our expression of faith. So it is worth giving some thought to the expression of faith you are making as a parent, and to the responsibilities you are taking on in deciding to baptise your baby.

The rite of infant baptism reminds mothers and fathers that in asking to have their child baptised, they are committing to raise their child in the practice of the faith. At the heart of this are the two great commandments that Jesus taught: love of God and love of neighbour (Mark 12:30-31).

The practice of the Catholic faith also includes:

▶ striving for lives of personal holiness.

▶ being faithful to the Gospel.

▶ upholding the values of the Beatitudes (Matthew 5:3-12).

▶ making Christ known to others.

▶ living out the Church's moral and social teaching.

▶ following an informed conscience.

- ▶ attending Mass on Sundays and Holy Days of Obligation.

- ▶ receiving the sacraments of reconciliation and Eucharist at least once annually.

- ▶ contributing to the material needs of the Church.

That, you might think, is a rather daunting list. But it is not as off-putting as it might seem because all the items are connected and flow naturally from one to another (much as the Ten Commandments flow into the two great commandments). Studying and learning the Gospel with an open heart, for example, is a way of being faithful to it. It is also a form of personal holiness, which deepens our understanding of the Church's moral and social teaching, and so on.

As with everything in this book, the key is to engage with it for yourself, and the best way to do that is through a combination of heartfelt prayer, honest reflection and open discussion.

## *Reflection*

Read the Beatitudes (Matthew 5:3-12) and meditate on how you can uphold their values. Think in terms of real-life examples. Identify someone you know who is "poor in spirit" and consider in what way might they be blessed? Who mourns and how might they be comforted? Could you play any part in blessing or comforting them? How can you impart these values to your children?

### A prayer for greater commitment

Dear Father, thank you for showing me how I can deepen my faith through motherhood. Help me to impart Gospel values, real holiness and love of you to my children. Amen.

## Catholic rituals, traditions and customs

The Catholic Church has many rituals, traditions and customs – some of which, it has to be said, are more widely observed than others. How (and whether) you introduce your children to them depends on your own familiarity with them. If you have learnt them from your own mother, they will probably be so ingrained that passing them on will be second nature. But even so, passing on the rituals and customs of our faith gives us an opportunity to understand them afresh for ourselves.

If they are unfamiliar to you, do not feel you need to know or understand everything – nobody does, or could do in a lifetime! It would be far better to embark on a learning adventure with your children. There are many good resources for adults and children – books, websites, DVDs and the like – that can help you to explore the faith from all angles, and your priest or a catechist should be more than happy to see you as a family and talk things through.

The main objective is to find the value, significance and relevance of these things for yourself and to help your children to do the same. Friday abstention from meat, for example, teaches us self-control and sacrifice, and also reminds us that we are spiritual, as well as physical, beings. In an age when we are used to having anything we want, exactly when we want it, could that be a good lesson for your children? However, if abstention is going to cause your child to be singled out at school as "different", you might decide to avoid encouraging it for now, or you may want to approach the subject in a different way. As ever, pray, think and talk it through, and you will come to make wise and informed choices.

If the Church's rituals, traditions and customs seem strange to you, please do not let that put you off the faith. However, it would be a mistake to dismiss them. They are ways in which generations of Catholics have connected their everyday lives with the divine, and they form a rich and wonderful faith heritage to pass on to the next generation.

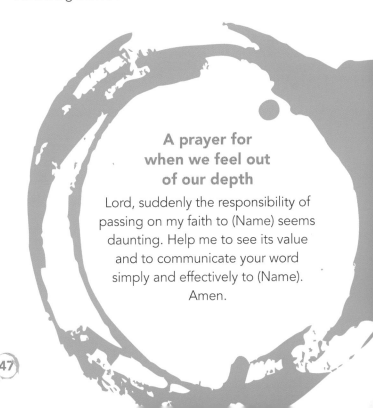

**A prayer for when we feel out of our depth**

Lord, suddenly the responsibility of passing on my faith to (Name) seems daunting. Help me to see its value and to communicate your word simply and effectively to (Name).
Amen.

## Mass

Sunday Mass is the most important and mysterious of the Christian rituals – a multi-layered celebration of what it is to follow Christ as his brothers and sisters.

The Mass is the pattern for our lives. At Mass we:

▶ gather before God as God's family.

▶ remember our failings and say sorry.

▶ listen to God's word and ponder its significance in our lives.

▶ affirm out loud our shared belief in God.

▶ ask God's help for all our needs.

▶ offer our gifts, the fruit of our toil, to our Lord and to our neighbour,

▶ bless and break bread together in honour of Jesus, who died and rose for us.

▶ share together Christ's body and blood, to be one with him and with each other.

▶ accept responsibility to take God's Good News to everyone we meet.

"We are more than just people who come to the same place each week to 'get Mass'. The priest begins with a greeting that the Lord is with us, and we are brothers and sisters in relationship. I think family life is a brilliant model for church life."

Veronica, mother of five

### A prayer for deeper faith

Lord God, there is something that draws me deeper into Catholic faith. Guide me in exploring the rituals and traditions and the great mystery of the Eucharist.
Amen.

Some young children can be seriously averse to going to Mass or prone to bad behaviour in church, which leaves parents with a number of dilemmas:

▶ How do we encourage children to do something that simply does not resonate with them?

▶ If we insist on them going to Mass do we risk putting them off church altogether in later life?

▶ How do we cope with the tantrums and tears that are so off-putting for other people in church?

▶ Should I bribe my children to behave well in church with sweets, toys and books?

Again, the answer depends on your circumstances and varies depending on the age of your children. Here are a few practical suggestions:

▶ Enlist the help of grandparents, aunts, uncles, friends, and the like. A grandmother can often make an experience special to a child in a way that a mother simply cannot!

▶ Ensure that anyone under eight has eaten a good breakfast before Mass – hunger can really exacerbate tantrums and tears!

▶ If necessary take a small soft (noise-free) toy as a distraction. Make it something special that your child only sees at Mass.

▶ For older children, read and discuss the Bible readings the day before so they engage with the words when they hear them in church.

▶ Before you go into church, have a word with your children so they know what to expect. Make sure they know that their "job" is to take part in singing and praying, and to be still and quiet at other times.

▶ Prepare them beforehand with a silent game. Who can see a cross, an altar, or a candle? You could give each a checklist and a pencil. Follow it up afterwards and make it a learning exercise.

▶ If a child really "kicks off", take him or her calmly and firmly outside until he or she has settled down. Return to your seat as soon as your child is calm again, or else he or she will start using it as a way of getting out of church.

▶ Make some time to talk to your children after Mass about what they saw and heard, and how they felt about it. Allow time for questions.

> "Whenever the opportunity arises: an incident at school between friends or something on the television, we try to **guide the children** from a biblical point of view and ask them, 'what would Jesus do?'"
>
> Niti, mother of three

## Catholic Social Teaching

As a mother wanting to pass on her faith to older children and young people, you might find that Catholic Social Teaching is a good introduction for them to get to know the Church and its teaching in a way that resonates for them. Catholic Social Teaching is challenging, radical and powerful – just like many young people! For this reason it often appeals to young people's strong sense of justice and makes good use of their energy and drive.

Catholic Social Teaching stems from the "great commandment" – to put God first, and to love your brother and sister as yourself. The issues covered can be broadly categorised into the following themes:

▶ Human dignity

▶ The dignity of work

▶ Solidarity

▶ Catholic teaching on poverty: a place at the table

▶ Faithful citizenship: a call to political responsibility

▶ Social justice

▶ Human and economic development

▶ Social sin

▶ Family life

> "'You shall love the Lord your God with all your heart, and with all your soul, and with all your mind.' This is the greatest and first commandment. And a second is like it: 'You shall love your neighbour as yourself.' On these two commandments hang all the law and the prophets."
>
> Matthew 22:37-40

## 66 TALKING IT THROUGH

- How did your faith journey begin?

- How would you describe your faith today?

- How do you share your faith with your children? *(Perhaps you are doing better than you think!)*

- Is there any aspect of the Catholic faith that you would not want to pass on? Would it be worth talking to your priest or a catechist about it?

- How important is it that children should have the freedom to question things for themselves? Explain your answer. *(Answer this honestly!)*

- How familiar are you with the rituals, traditions and symbolism of the Catholic faith? Do you feel you need to learn more? What resources could help you?

- Do the rites and customs make sense to you? If they do not, try to explain why you find them challenging. Have you ever questioned their value and significance? 99

"Children are never perfect plaster cherubs. But they do nevertheless have that clear and uncluttered vision of life which makes them ask the right questions."

Angela Ashwin, author

# Chapter six

# Weathering the storms

"Motherhood taught me some **humility:** I knew **I couldn't do it all** myself, it was beyond me."

Caroline, mother of eight

This chapter deals with some of the storms that mothers commonly face – from the day-to-day to the catastrophic. Of course the circumstances are unique to your situation, so it would be inappropriate to try to offer cut-and-dried solutions in this limited space. These are living, flesh-and-blood lessons in faith, love and compassion. But that does not mean that they are mere exercises. They are your lived experience and that of your family. In your darkest moments you may feel anger, humiliation, hostility or grief so raw that it seems unendurable. But – and this is not written lightly – God never sets us a challenge that we cannot rise to.

Just because something is covered here, it is not intended to imply that there is anything wrong with your situation or family. For example, the birth of a child with special needs presents parents with all kinds of tests, which might involve adopting a whole new way of living and being. This could be both immensely hard in the short term, but ultimately immeasurably rewarding.

If you are struggling with a particular set of circumstances, one of the first things to consider is what kind of support you need. Could talking it through with a priest, counsellor or therapist help, or does it require other help? Be realistic about your limitations and those of people around you; face the situation early on, seek appropriate support, and pray for guidance and wisdom.

## Managing the guilt

### "You cannot be without guilt, even when it is misplaced."

Julia, mother of two

Mothering is a life of perpetual motion, especially with young children. An ordinary day can feel like a non-stop hamster wheel of domestic chores – making breakfast, getting everyone dressed, doing the school run, going shopping, managing the finances, dealing with a bottomless laundry basket, drying tears, mediating squabbles, cooking meal after meal – and the house just isn't going to clean itself, you know.

It has been estimated that the economic value of all the work a mother does in the first eighteen years of her child's life is over £1.4 million – and that excludes any

salary she brings home. What is more, for all the feminist revolution, it has to be said that many women still take primary responsibility for household chores. It is estimated that women spend two hundred and fifty percent more time than men on cooking, washing up, cleaning and ironing, as well as forty percent more time caring for their children.

So when life is so relentlessly busy, even the most organised mother will inevitably become over-tired, stressed and discouraged from time to time, and lose a sense of the bigger picture. A sense of guilt seems to go with the territory – both with being a mother and with being Catholic. In itself, guilt can be destructive – sapping us of energy and self-confidence – so there is a real need to remember that being a "good enough" mother really is good enough.

Here are some suggestions, hints and tips on managing guilt:

▶ It is not always healthy for children to have perfect parents. Children need to know how injustice feels and to witness how adults say sorry and make up for their mistakes.

▶ It is not healthy for children to have everything they need or want, exactly when they need or want it. Going without from time to time is no bad thing.

▶ Children need their parents' time and attention more than the latest mobile phone, gadget or game.

- At the same time, children need boundaries and to learn to give adults space and time.

- When you catch yourself feeling guilty, get into the habit of saying a quick prayer or taking a few breaths, and move on.

- Try not to feel guilty about feeling guilty, or you will get stuck in a vicious cycle of blaming yourself.

- Do your best; admit your failings and do not harbour regrets.

- Seek out good friends with whom you can share your troubles and laugh.

- When things get really chaotic, remember that chaos was the starting point from which God created the universe.

### A prayer for an exhausted mother

Dear Lord, I am shattered. Give me strength to get through this and recover. Help me to keep my cool and not to say anything unkind. Be with me in all that I must still do, so that I may do it lovingly.
Amen.

### Heartbeat meditation

Close your eyes and take a few breaths. Know that you are surrounded and supported by the Holy Spirit, and that what you are doing is good enough. Breathe in that knowledge and let go of the guilt with the out breath.

"Guilt? Children are masters at making you feel guilty. I just try to move on. There's always something else to feel bad about just around the corner."

Katie, mother of four

## Relationship wobbles

It is a rare relationship in which a couple does not stare into the abyss at some point. When you go through relationship problems – whether it is a storm in a teacup or a serious, damaging breach of trust – one of your concerns will surely be how it is affecting the children.

The Catholic Church considers the bond of marriage to be sacred – something which cannot be broken with temporal laws. This can raise ethical dilemmas for everyone when, for example, infidelity is involved. So be prepared to talk it through, and to admit when you have not got the answers.

Even if a relationship problem affects a couple outside your immediate family (such as an uncle or aunt), children and young people of all ages can be deeply affected and troubled. So be aware of the ripple effect, be ready and willing to talk, and bear in mind that the effects of divorce or separation can be deeper and more lasting than a child or young person might let on.

## My baby's giving me the blues

These days postnatal depression is much more talked about than it once was, and hopefully health workers will have advised you about it. It is worth restating that it affects so many new mums in ways that are sometimes difficult to recognise. So if you feel isolated (even if you are surrounded by people and support), teary, down, angry, overwhelmed, unable to cope or bond with your baby, please treat it as an urgent warning sign and seek help.

While your parish priest may be able to offer an ear, it is important that you seek help from a medical professional, starting with your GP.

## Challenging lifestyles

However prepared we think we are to weather the storms of motherhood, the situations our children confront us with can stop us in our tracks and turn all our ideas about the future upside down. How you respond, of course, depends very much on your individual circumstances.

Whatever your real-life situation, one of the worst things you can do is try to force yourself to like or agree with anything, because that way you will only set up an inner conflict. On the other hand, you do not want to start an argument that could cause real damage at an already difficult time, or become so entrenched in disapproval that you drive a wedge between you and your child.

So rather than trying to force yourself or anyone else to change, pray for guidance. Ask God to teach you how to accept the situation just as it is (that means accepting the reality – not necessarily agreeing with it). Talk to a priest or counsellor if you think it will help, and practise seeing each and every person as Jesus does. Above all, pray that God will help you to turn every problem and challenge you face into an opportunity for spiritual growth, so that you can learn unconditional love as Jesus taught it.

### The serenity prayer

God, grant me the serenity to
accept the things I cannot change,
The courage to change the things I can,
And wisdom to know the difference.
Amen.

## 66 TALKING IT THROUGH

- What lifestyles have you come across that conflicted with your ethics and values?

- What shocked you?

- What inspired you?

- How do you think other people view your lifestyle?

- How can we explain our own and other people's lifestyle choices to our children? 99

### Bad behaviour

We talk about our "little angels", but of course it is highly unlikely that apart from the Virgin Mary any mother in the history of the world has ever weathered the storms of motherhood without experiencing disobedience or bad behaviour in some form. From a toddler's tantrums to a troubled teenager – caring for this person whom we love unconditionally, yet who may be difficult to like, is one of the great challenges of motherhood.

One of the most harmful and upsetting behavioural issues is when our children reject us. Because they know us so well, they know precisely how to belittle or demean us. To weather these storms, it is really important to have a strong sense of self-worth, and to seek out strong allies who can support you.

## 66 TALKING IT THROUGH

- Does your child reject you sometimes? If so how do you react?

- How can you be clear with your child about what is acceptable and what is not?

- What can you do to keep a sense of self-worth? Who can you turn to? 99

"What is most burdensome in life is a lack of love. It weighs upon us never to receive a smile, not to be welcomed. Certain silences are oppressive, even at times within families, between husbands and wives, between parents and children, among siblings. Without love, the burden becomes even heavier, intolerable."

Pope Francis

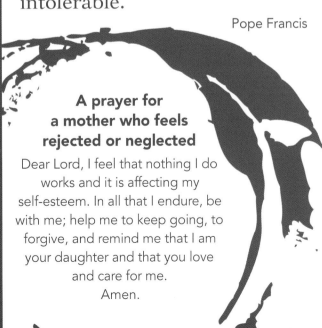

**A prayer for a mother who feels rejected or neglected**

Dear Lord, I feel that nothing I do works and it is affecting my self-esteem. In all that I endure, be with me; help me to keep going, to forgive, and remind me that I am your daughter and that you love and care for me.
Amen.

## Special needs

*"God loves each of us as if there were only one of us."*

St Augustine

The birth of a child who needs specialist medical or educational help can present unique challenges for even the best-prepared, best-supported, most loving family.

If you have a child with special needs, you will hopefully be supported by your doctor and other professionals – and they can certainly help you in practical ways more than this book can. But it is worth saying that the Church is hugely supportive in this kind of situation. There are some helpful resources available, and catechists who are skilled in all aspects of working with children who have special needs. Also, remember that the sacraments can be hugely helpful – for parents, for children and for siblings. So it is a very good idea to find out what support is available through your parish or diocese, or even at a national level.

**A prayer for the mother of a child with special needs**

Lord, as your creation, each of us is beautiful. Thank you for the unique gift and enrichment that this adorable child brings to our family. I pray for the strength and resources to be fully supportive, and the grace to love unconditionally.
Amen.

## Step, adoption and foster relationships

Families are more complex these days, and it is not at all unusual to have step, adoption or foster relationships alongside biological relationships – or any combination of the above.

Mothering a child you are not biologically linked to can be wonderful and rewarding, but it is very rarely a situation that is harmonious from the outset. If you are in this kind of situation you are hopefully receiving support from professional agencies, and there should be help available through your parish as well.

Do not panic if, at first, you find it difficult to bond with a step, foster or adopted child. Fighting your feelings will only set up an inner conflict. You are facing an awesome responsibility, possibly in a situation which is not of your choosing. Whatever the circumstances, know that the weight of responsibility and the awareness of the commitment you are making can, of itself, set up all kinds of wobbles and doubts. So go easy on yourself and channel your energy into being fair, setting boundaries, and getting to know the child as a son or daughter of God.

"Do not waste time bothering whether you 'love' your neighbour; act as if you did. As soon as we do this we find one of the great secrets. When you are behaving as if you loved someone, you will presently come to love him."

C. S. Lewis

## Sickness, bereavement and estrangement

If you have a serious illness or have experienced loss or separation in your family, no book can be a substitute for human comfort and the consolation of the Holy Spirit. There are times when the only thing to do is to watch and wait, as Mary did at the foot of the cross (as we saw in Chapter two). There are times when we just have to haul ourselves out of the hole and ask for help. At such dark times, this can be one of the greatest expressions of faith that anyone makes – ever!

Whatever your pain, and however isolated you feel in it, please seek help and support. If you do not find it at first, keep searching. Practise kindness and compassion towards anyone who is unable to respond in exactly the way you think they should, but do not beat yourself up when you feel anything but kind. Go easy on yourself, and bear in mind that anger, depression and a sense of isolation are by-products of grief. There are many wonderful resources out there – Christian, Catholic and non-religious, as well as many support groups for people who have been through something similar.

### A prayer for when a child is ill

Loving God, my baby is sick and suffering. Keep us safe while we get through this. Help me to keep calm and hopeful. Comfort us with your loving presence. And please God, make my child well again.
Amen.

## 66 TALKING IT THROUGH

- How did you feel when your child was unwell?

- When and how have you experienced loss? How did you cope? Did you lose sight of God and your faith? If so, was it restored, and how? 99

"In sad times I go to Mass and cry, and take comfort from the congregation."

Jane, mother of three

### A prayer at a time of loss

Heavenly Father, I trust you to know how I feel right now. It hurts so badly I can hardly bear it. Why did this have to happen? What am I going to do now? Out of the depths I cry to you, O Lord. Lord, hear my prayer and send your Spirit to comfort me.
Amen.

# Chapter seven

# Supporting and being supported

"Often the church uses 'familial' language, and talks about brothers and sisters and 'mother Church' and 'Father God'. I think my lived experience in family life as a mum gives me insights into what the Church really could be if it took these words describing our relationships seriously!"

Veronica, mother of five

They say it takes a village to raise a child. As Catholics we could think of that in terms of the Church – both at a local level (your parish community) and the worldwide Catholic Church. Both these structures, in different ways, have an active interest in helping you to raise a happy, healthy child who is firm in faith and active in Church life. This is not for the sake of keeping up numbers or swelling the congregation, but in order to do God's work in the world.

Very often the best thing a parish provides is very simply a network of people who share your values and outlook. None of us can mother alone – and it helps enormously to connect with women who are also mothering from a Catholic perspective.

Although the parish priest generally sets the tone of parish life, keeping a community vibrant is actually everyone's responsibility. How active a role you are able to play will of course depend on the ages of your children and your other responsibilities.

If your children attend a Catholic school, you can really make a significant contribution to the life of the school. Yes, it is time-consuming, but it can be hugely rewarding. Motherhood is all about adjusting and re-adjusting your priorities, so give some thought as to whether you can get more involved.

These days, parishes are recognising more and more the huge benefits of being family-friendly, inclusive and welcoming. But if you find that your parish is behind the times and you want to organise something, here are some of the possibilities:

▶ A children's Liturgy of the Word during Sunday Mass.

▶ A child-friendly mothers' prayer or discussion group – either in the church or at a parishioner's home.

▶ A toddler group or parents' association.

▶ Involvement in Catholic women's organisations – such as the Union of Catholic Mothers and the Catholic Women's League – and encouraging other women to become involved.

▶ Social events such as shopping or a cinema trip, or coffee morning.

▶ Providing a "hub" of support for both mothers and fathers. For example, encouraging and helping them to access parenting programmes, setting up a small library of resources for parents, or organising a children's "hand-me-down clothes" event.

▶ Providing opportunities for parents to reflect on family spirituality when their children are preparing to receive the sacraments.

▶ Encouraging your church to celebrate the contribution that mothers make to the life and mission of the Church on occasions such as Mothering Sunday.

▶ Organising fundraising or charitable activities within your church.

▶ Reaching out to help those in need in the wider community. This might mean providing respite care for mothers of children with special needs, or reaching out to women experiencing unwanted pregnancy, or domestic abuse, or families living in poverty in your local area.

If nothing like this exists in your parish, it just takes one or two energetic individuals to make a start. Could you be one of them? Here are some suggestions, hints and tips as to how you could go about it:

▶ Do not be retiring. People love good ideas and the chances are that they are just waiting for someone else to initiate it. Talk to the priest and check what has

already been tried and shown not to work (but do not necessarily let that put you off).

▶ Start small. Make sure that the workload it will involve is manageable – you can always scale it up. Remember that you will probably end up doing most of the work, at least at first.

▶ Get a good team together to make it happen. The parish priest might know who would be interested in taking part in your initiative, or you could put a notice in the parish newsletter.

▶ Be clear about your role, your strengths and limitations. You might be good at administration, for example, but not at being a group leader.

That is not to say that you should not try new things or challenge yourself, but do not get lumbered with everything just because it was your original idea.

▶ Learn how to delegate and involve other people in meaningful ways. Think and pray about people's strengths and limitations, and work with them. Keep in mind the parable of the talents (Matthew 25:14-30).

▶ Remember to keep the "fun" in "fundraising".

▶ When disagreements and differences happen (which they do, often), do not let them fester. Encourage open discussion and practise humility and honesty. If it is appropriate, invite people to get together to talk and pray about the situation.

▶ Find out what church and diocesan resources are available to help your project. Could a neighbouring parish take part or play a supportive role?

▶ Use it as an opportunity for outreach into the local community. Find out if you could work in partnership with a local community organisation, or if you know any individuals who would be prepared to help.

▶ Take any legal requirements – for example, health and safety – extremely seriously, and let the appropriate people know your plans. Your parish or diocese will have ample resources and guidance available.

## " TALKING IT THROUGH

- How does the Church (for example your children's school or your parish) support you in your mothering?

- As a mother what do you think you bring to the life of the wider Church?

### A prayer for starting an initiative

Lord God, give me energy, enthusiasm and vitality to do this. Help me to build a good team and to find a way of working with other people. Help us all to keep in mind that we are doing this for your greater glory.
Amen.

- Is there anything you can do to make sure mothers feel supported in your parish?

- Is there a project or initiative you would like to get going? If so, in what way would it work for God's greater glory? Could it bring together members of your church community, or be an opportunity for outreach? ,,

# Chapter eight

# Mothers in scripture

> "His mother treasured all these things in her heart. And Jesus increased in wisdom and in years, and in divine and human favour."
>
> Luke 2:51-52

The experiences and challenges of motherhood feature throughout the scriptures. The book of Genesis alone offers us Sarah, who waited until her old age for Isaac to be born; Hagar, who was cast out into the wilderness with her son Ishmael; Rebekah, whose twin sons Esau and Jacob fought even within her womb; sisters Rachel and Leah, both wives to Jacob and mothers of his children; and Tamar, who tricked her father-in-law Judah so that she could conceive the children of her late husband.

Tamar is listed among the ancestors of Jesus. Also mentioned in Matthew's Gospel as part of his family tree are Rahab, Ruth and Bathsheba, the wife of Uriah. These mothers were not especially respectable. Rahab was a Canaanite prostitute. Ruth seduced an old, wealthy relative in order to marry him. Bathsheba "manoeuvred" to obtain the throne for her son, who was not next in line. Yet these women are honoured ancestors of Jesus. Their stories tell us that God is happy to work through even the most marginalised women with the most unconventional lifestyles and behaviour.

Luke's Gospel alludes to the kind of mothering that Mary provided during the hidden years of Jesus' childhood and young adulthood. We know that she enjoyed the support of a husband for at least the first twelve years or so, but thereafter we cannot be sure. We can be sure though that her mothering was critical in raising Jesus to be a fully rounded person, capable of carrying out his mission as God's Son.

Dante Gabriel Rossetti, *La Pia de Tolomei*

# Mothers in the Bible

Here are some other mothers from the Bible:

**Eve** mother of Cain and Abel (Genesis 2:22-4:17)

Eve is the name of the first woman, the wife of Adam, the mother of Cain, Abel and Seth. Following their disobedience, Adam and Eve immediately lose the grace of original holiness. "The harmony in which they had found themselves, thanks to original justice, is now destroyed… the union of man and woman becomes subject to tensions" (*Catechism of the Catholic Church*, 400). As a mother, Eve's suffering must have been incalculable when one son murdered another.

**Sarah** mother of Isaac (Genesis 18:1-15; 21:1-7)

One of the most important women in the Bible, Sarah was the wife of Abraham and mother of the nation of Israel. Yet at first she was barren and only conceived in old age through a miracle. Her faith is an example for every mother who has to wait for God to act.

**Rebekah** mother of Esau and Jacob (Genesis 25:20-34; 27:1-45)

Like her mother-in-law Sarah, Rebekah was barren. When Isaac prayed for her, God opened her womb and she conceived and gave birth to twin sons, Esau and Jacob. In an age when women were typically submissive, she took matters into her own hands, with mixed results.

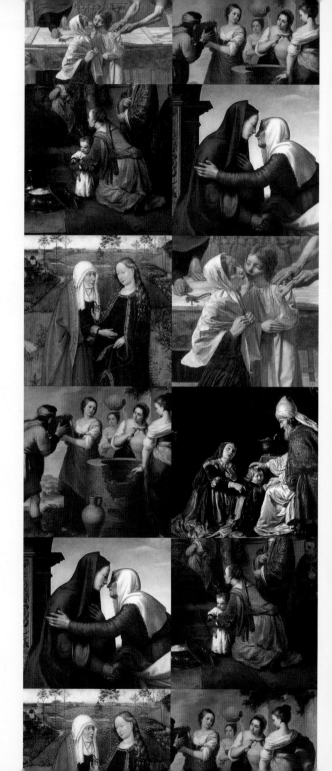

**Jochebed** mother of Aaron, Moses and Miriam (Exodus 2:1-10; 6:20; Numbers 26:59)

Her story is both heart-rending and joyous. To avoid the slaughter of Hebrew boys, Jochebed set her baby adrift on the River Nile in a papyrus basket. That baby – Moses – was discovered by Pharaoh's daughter, and thanks to the ingenuity of his sister Miriam, Jochebed ended up becoming nurse to her own son. Her story shows how God can turn even the bleakest of situations around.

**Naomi** mother Mahlon and Chilion (Ruth)

When she lost her husband and her sons, her daughters-in-law – particularly Ruth – became her family. She had dark times and ended up raising her step-grandson. Naomi's bittersweet story is an inspiration for anyone dealing with loss in motherhood.

**Hannah** mother of Samuel (1 Samuel 1; 2:21)

Like Sarah and Rebekah, Hannah knew what it meant to suffer years of barrenness, with the added insult of being taunted by her husband's other wife. But she never gave up. When God finally answered her prayers and she gave birth to Samuel, she kept her promise to give her son as someone wholly dedicated to God. After that God blessed her with five more children. From Hannah we can learn never to give up asking God for what we want.

**Elizabeth** mother of John the Baptist (Luke 1:5-7. 24-25. 39-45. 57-60)

Elizabeth conceived in advanced years. In contrast with her sceptical husband Zechariah, Elizabeth demonstrated faith, gratitude and joy, which was complete when her cousin Mary visited her, pregnant with the Messiah. Her son, John the Baptist, became the greatest prophet.

> "And through it all Mary of Nazareth kept pondering, kept thinking about the meaning of her life and the lives of those she loved, kept walking her journey of faith with God."
>
> Elizabeth Johnson,
> *Truly our Sister:*
> *A Theology of Mary in the*
> *Communion of Saints*

### A prayer for all mothers

Loving God, thank you for these examples of real motherhood. Thank you for these mothers, and for all those I know. Thank you for my own mother, and for bestowing on me the gift of motherhood.
Amen.

# A prayer for mothers

When the faith of the disciples was most tested by difficulties and uncertainties, Jesus entrusted them to Mary, who was the first to believe, and whose faith had never failed.

Mary became our Mother when she lost her divine Son. Her sorrowing heart was enlarged to make room for all of us, whether "good" or "bad", and she loves us as she loves Jesus.

At the wedding at Cana in Galilee, Mary's faith enabled the wonders of God to be displayed in the world; at Calvary she kept alive the flame of faith in the resurrection of her Son... Mary becomes, in this way, a source of hope and true joy!

The Mother of the Redeemer goes before us and continually strengthens us in faith, in our vocation and in our mission.

By her example of humility and openness to God's will, she helps us to transmit our faith, in a joyful proclamation of the Gospel, to all, without reservation.

To her, let us entrust our journey of faith, the desires of our heart, our needs and the needs of the whole world, especially of those who hunger and thirst for justice and peace, and for God.

Mother of God! Pray for us.
Amen.

Pope Francis
1 January 2014
Solemnity of Mary, Mother of God

Gerard David, *The Marriage at Cana*

# Further reading
## *and resources*

### Websites

Initiatives of the Catholic Bishops' Conference of England and Wales

**www.familias-ew.org.uk**
A list of the diocesan coordinators of family ministry. There are also resources for parishes, family spirituality and passing on the faith.

**www.catholicparenting.info**
Links to local Catholic parenting support.

**www.cedar.uk.net**
Resources for Catholics experiencing domestic abuse.

**www.mentalhealthproject.co.uk**
Resources generated by Catholic mental health projects.

### Other websites:

**www.theucm.co.uk**
Website of the Union of Catholic Mothers.

**www.mothersprayers.org**
Website of the Mothers' Prayers movement.

**www.familycaring.co.uk**
Low-cost community resources for reflecting on parenting skills.

**www.1277.org.uk**
Ecumenical website supporting Christian toddler groups.

**http://thecoupleconnection.net**
Support for couples when they become parents.

**www.catholicmom.com**
American website for Catholic mothers.

**www.catholicsocialteaching.org.uk**
An introduction to Catholic Social Teaching.

**www.afteradoption.org.uk**
Voluntary adoption agency working throughout England and Wales to help all those affected by adoption.

### FURTHER READING
### Books by Redemptorist Publications:

**Bairbre Cahill,** *Family Spirituality: God amongst the Pots and Pans* (2012).

*Being a Catholic Grandmother* (2014).

**Mares Walter,** *Faith for the Future: an Illustrated Catechism of Catholic Belief in Words and Pictures* (1997; sixth printing, 2008).

*I Belong* series (with children's, leader's and parent's guides):
*I Belong, I Belong Special, I Belong Confirmation* and *I Belong Common Worship.*